THE RIVER CLYDE

from the Source to the Sea

THE RIVER CLYDE
from the Source to the Sea

KEITH FERGUS
TEXT BY IAN R. MITCHELL

breedon **books**
PUBLISHING

I would like to thank my parents and my wife Helen for their belief and encouragement in my pursuit of the perfect photograph (I have yet to take it). Also to Helen for her incredibly understanding attitude throughout – the vagaries of the Scottish weather could often mean me being out the door, camera in hand, at a moment's notice.

I would also like to thank Ian, who on initial contact did not know me from Adam, but agreed to meet me anyway. His help and advice throughout has been invaluable. His superb text only goes to underline why I wanted him on board in the first place.

I must also thank all at Breedon Books who obviously saw something in the idea of a book on the River Clyde and, again, their help and advice has been greatly appreciated.

Finally, I would like to thank my two wonderful children, Kyla and Cameron, for simply always putting a smile on my face.

Keith Fergus 2008

Dramatic early morning skies greet the River Clyde at Carstairs Junction.

First published in Great Britain in 2008
by The Breedon Books Publishing Company Limited,
Breedon House, 3 The Parker Centre, Derby DE21 4SZ.

© Keith Fergus and Ian R. Mitchell, 2008.

ISBN 978-1-85983-666-8

Printed and bound in Europe

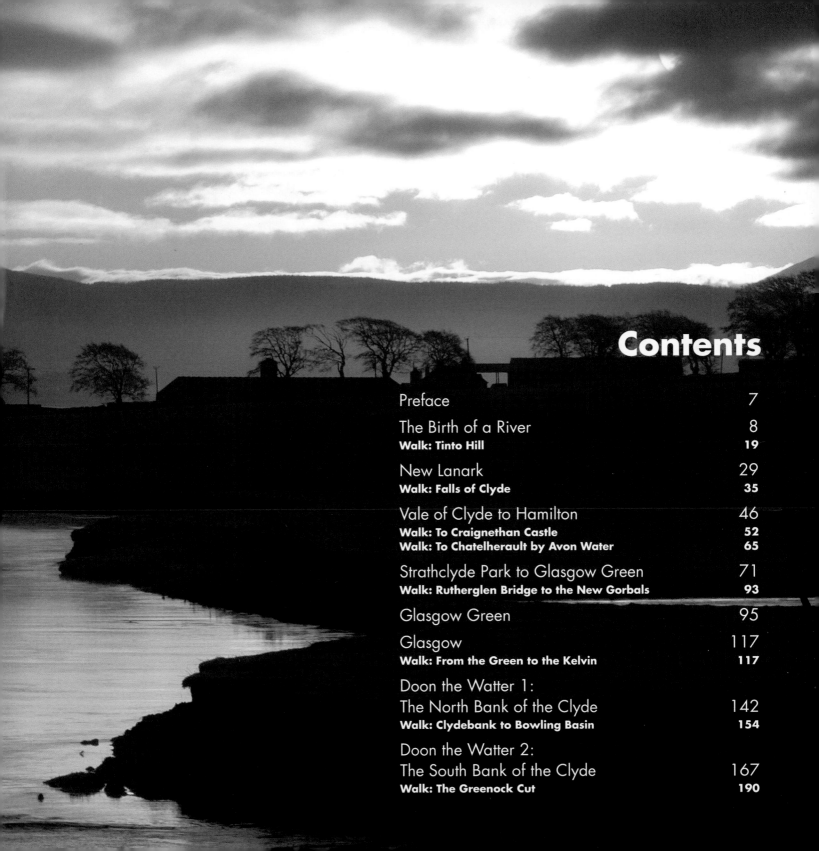

Contents

Preface

The mention of the River Clyde throughout the world will probably evoke images of the waterway's great commercial past, when the ships, locomotives and industrial machinery manufactured on its banks were sent to all corners of the globe. This is a now largely vanished tradition to which the Clyde can still relate with pride, but even in its industrial heyday, only a small part of the banks of the Clyde was devoted to industrial production. Most of Clydeside, then and now, consists of some of the grandest and most varied scenery to grace any of Scotland's rivers.

Starting in the wild high hills of the Upper Ward of Lanarkshire, the Clyde flows through some extremely sparsely populated territory, where in past times the footsteps of the Romans, the Reivers and the Covenanters trod. It then drops swiftly into Scotland's Garden of Eden, the former fruit-growing Vale of Clyde, which is as sheltered and fertile as the previous territory is wild.

Even when the river enters urban Clydeside after the Vale, the towns of Motherwell and Hamilton are set well back from the river banks, and the Clyde wanders through pleasant parklands – and on finally reaching Glasgow the first sight is that of Glasgow Green. From the city on downriver the banks are more built up, but the river widens to give fine perspectives of the Renfrew Hills to the south and the Loch Lomond hills to the north, and down towards the Firth of Clyde and the Cowal hills.

All along the banks of the river there are wonderful oases of nature and wildlife (quite an achievement for a river declared officially 'dead' in the 1970s), the ruins of historical castles, as well as many fine heritage examples of the river's former industrial glory. Keith's picture folio of the Clyde, from its source to the sea, gives a marvellous impression of the river, and I am delighted to have been asked to provide the text to accompany these splendid images.

Ian R. Mitchell.

The Birth of a River

For a waterway that was to become for a while the world's greatest industrial river, the Clyde has a quiet beginning at a place called Watermeetings. Here the Daer Water and the Potrail Water join their modest forces to flow somewhat stronger, and a little downstream from Watermeetings the tiny Clydes Burn adds its flow to the joint watercourse, and probably added its name as well. We are in wild and remote country, the upper reaches of Lanarkshire, where the moors rise to meet the county border with Dumfriesshire, the hills around having rough Scots names like Cleuch, Dod, Law. This is a harsh, some might say bleak, country and the land itself is as difficult as the climate, with little arable ground and a very scattered population. But you do not need to look hard at certain seasons and in certain lights to see great beauty in this landscape, and you need only a curious eye to find the many traces around of the human passage that formed this landscape.

Autumn colours surround the Daer Water, one of the two infant tributaries of the River Clyde, near Watermeetings.

The second of the River Clyde's two infant tributaries, the Potrail Water, strikes her course through the undulating hills of South Lanarkshire.

The fortified remains of Glenlochar Bastle and the crisp clean waters of Glenlochar Burn.

Watermeetings.

Just north of Watermeetings is the Bastle of Glenochar, which forms an interesting side trip of about a mile's round walk from the main road. This remote farm from the 16th century and its fortified structure shows us that the Border Reivers who raided England from Scotland and vice versa reached much further in their quest for spoils than was once thought. This warfare was ended after 1603, when James VI became King of England as well as Scotland, and the Debatable Lands of the Borders were pacified. But other kings passed this way too. In 1507 James IV travelled through here on foot, following the pilgrim's route from Edinburgh to Whithorn, which threaded through the hills by the Daer Water to Durisdeer. Indeed, thousands of pilgrims in the Middle Ages travelled this way to Whithorn.

But these pilgrims were only following a far older route, much more of which must have been visible in their day than is to us. From Elvanfoot, three miles north of Watermeetings, it is possible to walk for several miles south on the old Roman Road. From Watermeetings it follows the Potrail not the Daer and is covered with tarmac till it comes to the farm of Overfingland. From there, south to the county border between Durisdeer Hill and Well Hill, the route of the road is easy to follow. From the latter vantage point the road can be seen descending into Dumfriesshire, and the outline of a Roman Fortlet just a mile away is clearly discernible.

The Roman Road and the River Clyde turn their backs on this wild upland region when they get to Elvanfoot, and the scenery softens just a little. Here both road and river dip swiftly under the thundering traffic of the M74 and the track of the main London to Glasgow railway line, then both are again lost in quiet backwaters like Crawford, Abington and Symington, typical of the charming towns of Upper Clydesdale. East and west of Symington lie two of Clydesdale's gems: the town of Biggar and the great bulk of Tinto Hill.

Glenlochar Bastle, a remote 16th-century farm, is situated in a wild and desolate spot.

The distinctive outline of Elvanfoot Church on a cold winter's morning.

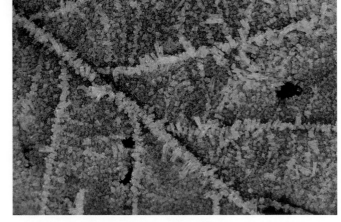

Left: A path leading to the quiet village of Crawford. There is much evidence of old Roman roads and settlements near here.

Frosted leaf.

The Clyde flows north, past the
rumbling traffic of the M74 and
the quiet village of Abington.

Previous page: A copse of Scots Pine stands
beside the Clyde near the village of Crawford.

Castle Hill above Crawford at dawn, one of the many wonderful vantage
points from which to witness the Clyde strike her course through the landscape.

The River Clyde begins her journey high in the hills of South Lanarkshire, and still bears witness to regular heavy snowfalls through the winter months.

The hardy sheep endure a tough existence when winter takes hold.

The striking red cairn of Tinto Hill, the culmination of a wonderful walk to her summit.

Right: Bog Cotton, surviving on the slopes of Tinto Hill.

Far right: Crowberry on the slopes of Tinto Hill.

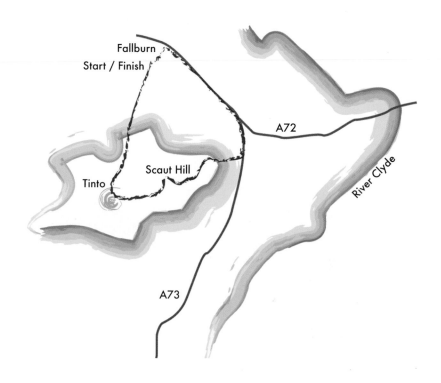

Walk: Tinto Hill

The conical Tinto is a conspicuous landmark in this farming region, and there is some suggestion that the name of the hill derives from its use by the Romans as a beacon post. Certainly, a Roman road passes the west flank of the hill, and there are suggestions that the huge cairn on the summit may be of Roman origin, though others think it is from an earlier period. The Tinto Hill Tearoom, near Fallburn by Thankerton, is the usual starting point for an ascent of Tinto, and a clear and sometimes boggy path leads over Totherin Hill to the summit. From the summit on a clear day the mountains of the Scottish Highlands and the Lake District can be seen. Nearer to hand, the Clyde courses its way north, and back to its source at Watermeetings. The return trip of about 7km has about 450m of ascent and takes a fairly leisurely three hours. If you do not mind a couple of miles on the road before arriving back at the tea room, it is possible to descend over Scaut Hill, above the remains of the quaintly-named Fatlips Castle below.

'London's big but Biggar's biggar', they are apt to say of this real gem of a town in Upper Clydesdale, though it stands a little over a mile from the river itself. It is a centre for a wide area, and a charming place to wander around, with its many cafés, shops and museums. Other towns may be book towns or fair trade towns, but Biggar is definitely a museum town. This area of Upper Clydesdale was one of the strongholds of the Covenanting movement in the 17th century, and at Greenhill (now within Biggar itself) a farmhouse from the period hosts an interesting collection relating to the so-called Killing Times.

Sunrise over Culter Fell and her outliers, from neighbouring Tinto Hill.

The gorgeous patterns and colours of lichen, Quothquan Law.

The distinctive whaleback contours of Tinto Hill from Quothquan Law, the Clyde meandering around her base.

The quiet village of Thankerton at dawn, from the slopes of the curiously named Quothquan Law.

Left and below: Approaching storm clouds hold the promise of more snow near Symington.

The warm glow of dawn reflecting from the River Clyde near Biggar.

Biggar's main attraction, however, is probably the Victorian Gasworks, now maintained by the National Museums of Scotland, and the last functioning one in the country with its original machinery from the 1830s. The Moat Park Heritage Centre tells of the town's connections with William Wallace, the Gladstone Court Museum explains the local origins of the famous Victorian Prime Minister's family, and at Brownsbank Cottage, a little outside the town, is an exhibition commemorating the long residence there of Hugh MacDiarmid, probably Scotland's greatest 20th-century poet.

The church steeple at Biggar, with the bulk of Tinto in the background.

'London's big, but Biggar's biggar' – winter sunshine strikes the charming high street of Biggar.

Dramatic early morning skies greet
the River Clyde at Carstairs Junction.

Winter grips the landscape at Hyndford Bridge – thick hoar frost clings to the fields and trees.

Hoar frost, Hyndford.

We can dally with delight at Biggar, but the Clyde hastens on northwards past the curiously named little hill of Quothquan Law to its junction with the Medwin Water. The ever-increasing waters flow past the railway junction at Carstairs, with its gloomy mental hospital on the hill behind, and take a westward turn towards the town of Lanark. At Hyndford Bridge the road to Lanark crosses the river, and we will follow and have a look at this small town, which was once the county seat of the whole of Lanarkshire.

The River Clyde flows under the striking bridge at Hyndford, and begins her journey towards Lanark.

Lanark has some wonderfully distinctive buildings, not least the old octagonal livestock market buildings. The steeple of St Mary's Church provides a lovely backdrop.

If Biggar is a museum town, Lanark is a market and fair town, still hosting both its unique Lanimer Fair in early June, a riding of the marches event, and the Whuppitie Scourie Fair in March. A festivity that no longer exists is the Lanark races, once one of Scotland's main events of its kind, but now commemorated only by the disused Lanark Race Course. Still there, however, are the buildings of the Lanark livestock market, and the town is still a major centre of agricultural sales. The town centre boasts a very wide street, which was traditionally the scene of its busy market place.

Lanark is purportedly where William Wallace raised the standard of revolt against the English in 1297 by attacking the local castle and killing the governor. The castle is no more, but a huge statue of William Wallace in the centre of the town commemorates this link. Lanark was to retain its rebellious traditions by being a centre of the Covenanting movement in the 17th century. Largely bypassed by the Industrial Revolution, Lanark declined in importance and became a sleepy backwater. However, events of international significance were to take place in nearby New Lanark.

The William Wallace statue, Lanark, supposedly where the iconic leader raised the standard against the English in 1297.

New Lanark

New Lanark, where Robert Owen, whose ideas were way ahead of their time, transformed the working conditions for men, women and children.

Robert Owen was born in Wales and, after a career in the English textile industry, took over the management of New Lanark Cotton Mills in 1800. Owen married the daughter of David Dale, the 'father of the Scottish textile industry', who had established the mills at New Lanark in 1785. The setting was beautiful, and so were the mill buildings, built in stone on neo-classical lines to imitate the Palladian mansions of the 18th-century aristocracy.

The villas of Owen and Dale stand opposite the workers' houses at New Lanark.

The original village store is still open for business.

Postbox.

Window detail.

Dale was a religiously-inspired 'model' employer, who provided schooling and housing for his workers. Owen built on Dale's foundations and made several changes for the better, improving sanitation and education, reducing child labour, and by providing a store where workers could buy cheap goods, and most notably in establishing the Institute for the Formation of Character, a social and cultural centre. This was started due to his belief that character was moulded by environment.

Models greeting you at the visitor centre, one of New Lanark's wonderful idiosyncrasies.

Opposite: The buildings of New Lanark retain their wonderful character, such as these rows of chimney pots.

Owen was to coin the word 'socialism' but New Lanark was still a thoroughly capitalist enterprise, though more endurable than most at the time. Owen was a ruthless disciplinarian who paid his workers 50p a week and made a profit from the housing at the mill and also from the store – which was a company store and not a co-operative. Owen's store was a great improvement on the Truck System, which operated in most workplaces at this time, forcing workers to buy at the company store at inflated prices; by contrast the New Lanark store was cheaper and used by people from Lanark itself. Thousands of mainly middle-class visitors flocked to New Lanark to see how capitalism could treat its workers well and still make a profit. In 1825 Owen sold out his share of the mill, having made over £1 million from it in a quarter of a century.

New Lanark, a designated UNESCO World Heritage Site and a major tourist attraction.

The mill continued production, even though its fortunes were in decline until the 1960s. By this time many of the factory buildings were ruinous, and depopulation had left much of the housing empty. An ugly scrap-metal business operated out of here in the 1970s. Then people began to move into and restore some of the housing, and attempts were made to develop the heritage potential of the site. Now the village is a bustling place, with a hotel and youth hostel, and many of the mill buildings, as well as the Institute for the Formation of Character, have been refurbished. These developments were crowned by the granting of UNESCO World Heritage Status to the village. Today New Lanark is fascinating, inspiring and even beautiful, and it is possibly the best example of a humanely run capitalist enterprise from the period of the Industrial Revolution.

The River Clyde is a great source of energy, powering homes and businesses.

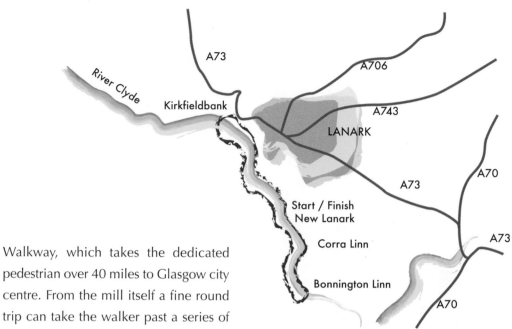

Walk: Falls of Clyde

Tourists came to see New Lanark from its foundation, but they also came to see the famed Falls of Clyde and were joined by poets including Wordsworth and painters such as Turner. Today the upper falls, Bonnington Linn, mark the beginning (or the end) of the Clyde Walkway, which takes the dedicated pedestrian over 40 miles to Glasgow city centre. From the mill itself a fine round trip can take the walker past a series of visual delights, with many points of historic interest. From the southern extremity of New Lanark village, the

Pine cone.

The Clyde Walkway
at New Lanark.

35

Waterfall detail near Bonnington Falls, New Lanark.

path follows the east bank of the Clyde through the Falls of Clyde Nature Reserve, which is one of the best places in Britain to see peregrine falcons. It passes the Corra Linn (Linn is Scots for waterfall), where the river narrows to a gorge and then continues to Bonnington Linn, where the river can be safely crossed.

Waterfall detail, New Lanark.

The Clyde Walkway offers peace and solitude as you wander beside the river.

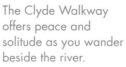

Heading northwards on the west bank of the Clyde takes you past the ruins of Corra Castle, a little beyond which is a splendid viewpoint over the whole New Lanark industrial enterprise. Its sandstone buildings are glorious, especially when seen in the setting sun; this is no 'dark satanic mill'.

The 27m-high Corra Linn, a spectacular sight at any time of year.

Damselflies are a common sight along the Clyde Valley throughout the months of May and June.

Autumn is possibly the best time to visit New Lanark as the colours along the Clyde Walkway are superb.

Fallen leaves on a bed of moss beside the Clyde Walkway, New Lanark.

Overleaf: Strong sunlight enhances the colours of the trees.

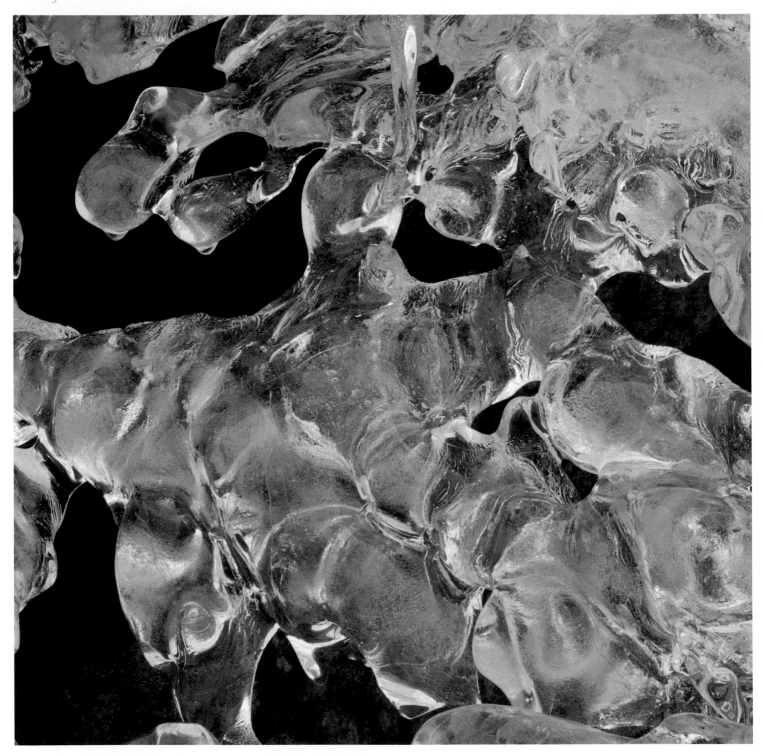

The displays of snowdrops can be wonderful as winter gives way to spring.

Left: Elaborate ice sculptures form
when water and cold temperatures
collide. Mother Nature at her finest.

Lesser Celandine.

At Clydesholm Bridge, dating from the late 17th century, the Clyde is crossed once more and the walkway is followed through Braxfield Park, back to the village of New Lanark again. The round distance is about six miles, the going easy, the views stunning and the whole walk a sheer delight. Allow three hours for the whole walk.

An abundance of wildflowers line the paths and woods of the Clyde Valley.

Right: Tree detail, New Lanark.

Wood anemone.

Vale of Clyde to Hamilton

The River Clyde constantly delights and surprises with its changes of scene, but none are so sudden as that downstream from Clydesholm Bridge. At Lanark and New Lanark we are still in the wild moorlands of the Upper Ward of Clydesdale. Below the bridge the river runs through a totally different landscape, one that has been described, due to its benign climate and fertility, as Scotland's 'Garden of Eden' – the sheltered fruit-growing Vale of Clyde.

It is legendary that the Romans introduced the cultivated apple into this Eden, not so much as fruit for themselves, more as food for their own favourite delicacy, the edible snail. For centuries this was the location of Scotland's main apple orchards, and though not what it was, the display of apple blossom here in April and May is a sight to behold. Other market gardening crops developed, including strawberries, and from the 1880s greenhouses sprouted like mushrooms as shelter for what became

Early morning spring sunshine casts long shadows at Hazelbank.

The old bridge at Kirkfieldbank is the first of many
wonderful bridges along the Vale of Clyde to cross the Clyde.

the most famous crop of the Vale, tomatoes. Many would claim that the small, hard and dark red Lanark tomato is the best-tasting of all.

For 50 years the Vale bloomed and boomed on this economy, and we are fortunate to have, in the *Linmill Stories* of Robert Maclennan, a picture of the Vale at its agricultural height around World War One, written in the Lanarkshire dialect. Sadly, that dialect is in decline and so too for many years was the economy of the Vale. But with the return to favour of local produce, a small revival in fruit farming has taken place over the last few years, though most of the greenhouses are gone and many of those remaining have become garden centres.

On the south bank of the river, the A72 passes through a trio of charming villages: Kirkfieldbank, Hazelbank and Crossford, where the houses have delightful flower-filled gardens in springtime and summer. At this time of year the villages, their pubs and tea rooms are full of tourists and day trippers, and the narrow road can be a bit traffic-choked. But from Clydesholm Bridge this throng can be avoided, if desired, by the use of the ever-present Clyde Walkway.

Waterfall, Clyde Valley.

What better way to spend an evening than a spot of fishing near Crossford?

Snowdrops, Hazelbank.

Late-evening sunshine adds to the tranquillity of Crossford, seen here from near the wonderfully-named Tillietudlem.

The beautifully designed bridge
spanning the Clyde at Crossford.

Craignethan Castle is ideally positioned for great views across the Clyde Valley.

Walk: To Craignethan Castle

From Clydesholm Bridge the walkway takes a north turn and soon comes to an even more spectacular viaduct – the great Scottish engineer Thomas Telford's Cartland Bridge over the Mouse Water. Built in the 1820s, it was Telford's highest bridge in Scotland, though one wonders what the justification was for the enormous expenditure it entailed, on a wee back road to the tiny village of Nemphlar which is next passed through. Then the walkway drops down to the Clyde and the tumultuous Stanebyres Linn and adjacent power station. A couple of miles of fine walking, high on the north bank with views across to the orchards on the other side, takes you to Crossford, and Crossford Bridge. From here the path climbs through the wooded defile of Lower Nethan Nature Reserve and comes in a short time to Craignethan Castle. One of the most finely situated and interesting castles in Scotland, it is protected on three sides by steep cliffs.

Like the wild moorlands around Lanark, the sweet fields of the Vale of

Clyde were strong for the Covenant in the 17th century and saw their share of bloodshed in those troubled times. Walter Scott's great novel *Old Mortality* is set in these parts, ranging from the battlefield of Drumclog in the moors beyond Lanark, through that town itself, and on down the Clyde to the bloody scenes at Bothwell Brig, where the 1679 rebellion ended. But the actions of Scott's novel centre around Tillietudlem

Castle, which is his disguise for the real-life Craignethan Castle.

The castle, built for Sir James Hamilton in about 1530, is well preserved and has a unique vaulted defensive gun chamber, the only such carponier in Scotland. The castle was surrendered and reduced after the 16th-century religious wars and did not figure in the troubles of the Covenanting era, despite Scott's account in *Old Mortality*.

Scott had many connections with the Vale of Clyde, a place he loved and often visited. His son-in-law, Lockhart, was a Clydesdale man, and Scott was offered a house at Craignethan by the admiring estate owner, an offer he declined.

The Clyde continues on its way south-westward to the village of Rosebank, which many would see as the jewel of the Vale; it was originally built as a

The Vale of Clyde is well known for its delicious crops of tomatoes.

Left: The Clyde Valley at dusk, with Tinto Hill's characteristic contours on the horizon.

Many of the greenhouses have fallen into disrepair but still have a certain appeal.

Overleaf: Early-morning sunshine casts the shadow of the bridge on the Clyde near Rosebank.

55

planned village for the workers in a local estate. On the north side of the river here, those wishing to pay homage to the great cartographer William Roy may chose to visit the monument at his birthplace, which takes the form of a trig point. Roy was a British army officer in the 18th century, who mapped the whole of the Scottish mainland after the 1745 Jacobite Rebellion. Roy is regarded as the pioneer of the later Ordnance Survey map system, and those trying to find Roy's memorial trig point would be well advised to have an OS map with them! (It is best approached from Carluke Station to the north.)

The Vale of Clyde ends as suddenly as it begins – the land opens out to the broader riparian scene below Garrion Bridge, and cultivated fields and pasturelands replace the fruit-growing terrain. But the landscape keeps its best till last in the village of Dalserf, a small hamlet built around a fine 17th-century church. The graveyard contains many interesting stones, including some of the Covenanting 'martyrs' and one of their persecutors, enemies united in death. Dalserf on a fine day in early summer is as near to Eden as it gets.

Below Garrion Bridge the farmland is much richer, and in the 18th and 19th centuries many fine mansions were built by the improving lairds. In the 1820s the

Fungi.

Left: The attractive 17th-century church at Dalserf. The graveyard contains stones attributed to the Covenanting martyrs.

Garrion Bridge.

Lockharts built Cambusnethan Priory (a mansion despite the name) above the Clyde here, and though it was damaged by a fire 30 years ago, the ruins make a very imposing sight. Further downriver was the Dalzell estate, which passed to the Hamiltons, the most powerful family around these parts. Beside the river is a graveyard, which contains many of the burial monuments of the family. After coming to the Baron's Haugh Nature Reserve, where a large loch is an important RSPB reserve, the fine stone viaduct of the Hamilton-Motherwell railway is passed under, and the scenery changes again as we enter urban Clydeside. From the Clyde here can be seen, on the breast of the hill, the stunning Motherwell Megaliths, a series of eye-catching high-rise flats that tower over the river below and form a fine skyscape as a backdrop to the Clyde. But Motherwell on the north bank of the river and Hamilton to the south keep well back from the Clyde itself, which still presents here a very rural prospect.

Right: The eye-catching remains of Cambusnethan Priory.

We have mentioned the Hamilton family, of whom it has been said that their history is the history of Scotland, so important a role did they formerly play. Here, around the town of the same name, we are in the heart of their kingdom. On the south side of the river, in Hamilton Low Parks, stands the Hamilton Mausoleum, built in 1858 for the 10th Duke of Hamilton. It is said to be the biggest mausoleum in the world, apart from the pyramids. This magnificent edifice is also reputed to have the longest echo – 15 seconds – of any building in Europe. But probably more significant is that it is now 15 feet lower than when it was built, due to land subsidence caused by coal mining. Much of the Hamilton family's wealth in the 19th century came from mining rights, and land subsidence caused by this led to the demolition of their splendid Hamilton Palace.

Hoar Frost near Dazell Nature Reserve.

The Motherwell Megaliths: as you approach the two large towns of Motherwell and Hamilton, these high-rise flats are the first sign of the River Clyde entering an urban landscape.

This was built to designs by David Hamilton (no relation) in the 1820s and demolished a century later in an event known locally as 'the miners' revenge', as the Hamiltons were not popular with the Lanarkshire colliers. One bugbear of the Hamiltons – and all mine owners – was Kier Hardie, who was based in Hamilton when he was attempting to organise trade unions among the Lanarkshire miners. But if the glories of the powerful Hamilton family can be seen only in their faded form in the Low Parks, a trip to Hamilton High Parks will show you an example of their glories restored, in the shape of the family's former hunting lodge of Chatelherault.

Swan, Dazell Nature Reserve.

Dazell Nature Reserve on the outskirts of Motherwell is a peaceful haven, rich in wildlife.

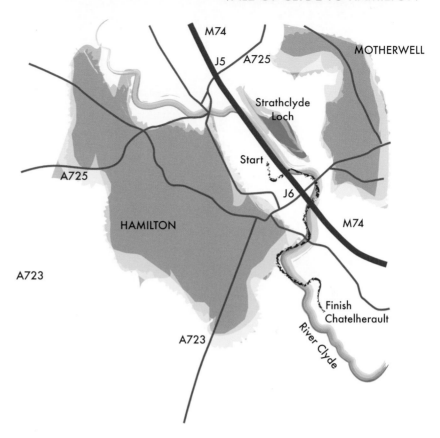

Walk: To Chatelherault by Avon Water

The Avon walkway can be picked up by heading north a short distance from the Hamilton mausoleum to the Clyde and then taking a right (south) turn along the river bank. The round trip from the mausoleum to the High Parks is about six miles, and it takes about three hours to walk. At Clyde Bridge, the track up the high wooded banks of the Avon is followed for a couple of miles, till the path breaks away from the Avon and climbs through the grounds of Chatelherault itself. Here you will see numbers of the famous Cadzow cattle,

bred by the Hamiltons since the Middle Ages and formerly hunted on special occasions. They are white, with black ears and feet, and sport large horns. They are a unique breed and are said to carry a strain from the original wild oxen of Europe.

The lodge itself was built from 1732–44 and is named after the French dukedom conferred on the Hamiltons a couple of centuries earlier. Its 280ft-long façade at the front was designed by William Adam and gives a slightly misleading impression of size and

magnificence. Much of this structure is actually a wall, and the living quarters behind are more modest but still very imposing. There were also extensive kennels, stables and estate buildings, and today Chatelherault has been fully restored as an excellent heritage and visitor centre. The Avon Walkway continues past Chatelherault and can be followed fruitfully for as long as the pedestrian desires. It passes the ruins of Cadzow Castle and the famous Cadzow oaks, reputed to be four or five centuries old.

Two of the huge old oaks on the grounds of Chateauherault.

Previous page: The sheer magnificence of Chateauherault.

One of the famous Cadzow Oaks, said to be many hundreds of years old.

Hamilton itself is an interesting town with many fine buildings, including William Adam's Old Parish Church of 1732. In a former Hamilton residence, just a little north of the mausoleum at the Cameronian roundabout, is a museum of the Cameronian regiment, raised in these parts. Hamilton was a centre of the Covenanting movement, and there is a Covenanters' Trail through the town.

The breathtaking Hamilton Mausoleum, is said to be the largest mausoleum in the world apart from the pyramids. It is also said to have the longest echo in Europe.

Low Parks Museum, one of the many lovely buildings to be found in Hamilton.

The local district museum is of interest mainly for its account of the coal industry, which dominated this area for almost two centuries. But the Lanarkshire coalfield, like the Hamiltons' wealth and lands, is no more.

Evening sunshine strikes the magnificent façade of Hamilton Town Hall, one of the many fine buildings within the town.

Strathclyde Park to Glasgow Green

Across the River Clyde from the Hamilton Low Parks lies Strathclyde Country Park, and the two large green areas together form a healthy lung between the urban communities of Motherwell and Hamilton. Strathclyde Park is based around a large artificial loch, below which lies a set of redundant coal mine workings and even a former pit village. Strathclyde Loch is a very popular centre for various watersports, and these activities are complemented by a cycle track along the south shore of the loch. For the pedestrian it is more pleasant to wander along the pathways that pass through a varied and wooded landscape on the north side of the loch. This way also lies a former Roman fort and the Bothwellhaugh Roman bath house, which was relocated closer to the fort when the loch was created and Strathclyde Park established. This military station was a relief barracks, located well behind the 'front line' of the Antonine Wall, and one where the legionaries came for rest and recreation. The fort also commanded the route back south through Clydesdale. The Clyde Walkway leaves the park by crossing the motorway to Raith Haugh (*haugh* is Scots for a low-lying piece of ground), a wetland that is ever alive with birdlife below the hum of traffic from the M74.

Cormorants taking it easy on Strathclyde Loch at dawn.

Looking towards Hamilton Mausoleum from Strathclyde Loch at dawn.

Previous Page: A beautifully still winter sunrise over Strathclyde Park's man-made loch.

Watersports are popular at Strathclyde Loch.

After Raith Haugh the river arrives at Bothwell Bridge, where the Clyde is crossed by a busy modern viaduct on the East Kilbride Expressway. A large monument stands nearer to where the original Bothwell Brig (now gone) was situated and commemorates the events of 1679, when a bloody battle was fought here for possession of the river crossing. The conflict at Bothwell Brig is brilliantly described in Walter Scott's novel *Old Mortality*, a book that should be read by anyone interested in the history of Clydesdale. After 1660, with the restoration of the Stuart monarchy, Episcopacy was imposed on Scotland, most of whose inhabitants preferred the Presbyterian form of religion – whose rites were outlawed on pain of death. Nowhere was stronger in support of these views than Lanarkshire, and many of the adherents of Presbyterianism – called Covenanters – engaged in a guerrilla war which eventually boiled over into armed rebellion in 1679. After an initial victory at Drumclog (also described in *Old Mortality*), the Covenanters were annihilated at Bothwell Brig, a battle followed by a disgraceful slaughter of the defeated and the pressing of many captives into slavery overseas.

The remains of Bothwellhaugh Roman Bath House.

Overleaf: Packhorse Bridge, Strathclyde Loch.

75

Previous page: The River Clyde rushes underneath Bothwell Bridge, near to where Covenanters were defeated in 1679.

The Clyde was, and is, crossed by many other bridges of historical importance in addition to Bothwell Brig. A little downstream stands what remains of Bothwell Viaduct, and anyone looking at the six massive stone piers (the deck has been removed) that straddle the Clyde here might think that he or she is in the presence of a Roman remain, a Pont du Gard of Caledonia, whereas it is in fact a Victorian construction, built to carry a now disused railway line. An example of more modern engineering, on a more modest scale, is the David Livingstone Memorial Bridge, a mile or so downriver at Blantyre. The bridge was named after the most famous son of Blantyre, and the David Livingstone Centre, run by the National Trust for Scotland, is located on the south bank of the Clyde at this point. Every year the Centre attracts visitors from around the globe paying homage to a remarkable man, virtually a secular saint in his Victorian lifetime and someone whose reputation is still high today.

David Livingstone Memorial Bridge, Blantyre.

Early-morning light catches the impressive building of the David Livingstone Centre, now owned by the National Trust for Scotland.

Monument to the missionary David Livingstone, who was born in Blantyre.

In 1785 David Dale (the founder of New Lanark mills) established another cotton mill in Blantyre, later selling it to Henry Monteith of Glasgow. Here in 1813, in a one-roomed tenement in Shuttle Row, Livingstone was born, and at the age of 10 he started in the mill, working a 14-hour day. He was able to educate himself despite all objective difficulties and later studied medicine at Glasgow University before becoming a missionary in Africa. The capital of

79

Monument to Blantyre's most famous son, David Livingstone.

present-day Malawi, Blantyre, is named in his honour. The Victorians admired Livingstone primarily for his Christian missionary activities, though the modern view tends to argue that he was rather ineffectual in that sphere and that his main achievements were as an explorer and as a publicist about, and campaigner against, the slave trade.

The Blantyre textile mill has long been demolished and is now an attractive park where a statue of Livingston stands, but the row of workers' housing in which the great man was born is still there and can be visited. Blantyre was a centre of the Lanarkshire mining industry for many years, until the last coal-winning activity ceased in the 1980s. It was also the scene of Scotland's worst-ever mining disaster in 1877, when 207 men were killed in an underground explosion.

Memorial to Scotland's worst mining disaster, High Blantyre.

Despite the revelation of many breaches of safety regulations at a public inquiry, the local MP failed to get Parliament to prosecute the mine owners. Though the coal mines are all gone, a fine memorial to the Blantyre disaster stands about two miles away at High Blantyre. It reminds us that while Livingstone was campaigning against abuses of human rights in darkest Africa, nearer to home human greed was responsible for equally culpable acts.

One of the most pleasant and popular parts of the Clyde Walkway is that which goes from Blantyre to Uddingston, a distance of just over a couple of miles through wooded riverscapes. In spring the displays of bluebells here are quite dazzling.

Bothwell Woods has a wonderful show of bluebells every year.

Wild garlic.

Wild garlic (ransoms) and bluebells, Bothwell.

The Clyde Walkway between Blantyre and Bothwell is a wonderful way to spend a few hours in the spring.

As you enter Bothwell Woods, you can always smell the garlic before you see it.

The sandstone of Bothwell Castle, burning red in the light of dawn.

About halfway along this section you come to the extensive Bothwell Woods and one of the jewels of the Clyde, Bothwell Castle. This is especially dramatic when its remains catch the rising and setting sun and the red sandstone appears to be on fire. Dating from the 13th century, the massive fortified structure is one of the finest examples of Scottish medieval secular architecture. The main tower is a massive keep, or donjon, and is the oldest part of the structure, and possibly part of a much larger structure of which only the foundations now remain. The castle figured prominently in the Wars of Independence, when it changed hands several times before being partially destroyed by the Scots themselves. It passed into the Douglas family, who repaired and extended the buildings. Military developments made such huge structures redundant, and over several centuries the castle decayed. Today it is cared for by Historic Scotland.

Right: The dramatic remains of Bothwell Castle.

Uddingston Viaduct is another striking crossing of the Clyde. It was originally built in 1848 by the Caledonian Railway Company and was subsequently made a double viaduct: both still stand, though only one deck is now in use. Uddingston itself is a pleasant town, and is mainly a commuter village for Glasgow with many substantial Victorian and Edwardian villas. It is the location of one of the few remaining manufacturing locations of any size on Clydeside, the Tunnock's bakery factory, dating from the 1890s. Tunnock's 700 workers make the much-loved caramel wafers, macaroon bars and teacakes. In Uddingston you might be lucky enough to see one of the firm's attractive antique delivery vans leaving the factory.

Uddingston Viaduct.

Downriver from Uddingston, the river soon comes to Carmyle, which lies within the boundaries of Glasgow itself, just after the disused Carmyle viaduct is passed. A charming curved weir on the river here provides a foreground to the disused railway viaduct. Downriver for a couple of miles, we are in the heart of what was formerly a heavy industrial area, with iron and steel works predominating. Almost all of this activity is now gone and has been replaced by modern industrial estates, housing or new motorways.

Despite this industrial past there are many interesting sights between Carmyle and Glasgow Green, where the Clyde Walkway wanders along the bends of the Clyde. Most of the industrial estates and roadways are invisible due to the tree cover on the river banks, and it is often difficult to believe the busy city is just a few hundred yards away. Part of the delight is the twisting nature of the trail; often you think you are walking back to where you came from, as landmarks appear, disappear and re-appear with the river bends. Amazingly, in the 1970s it was proposed to conduit these meanders in the river and build a motorway into central Glasgow over the buried Clyde. This part of the river is very popular with boaters, and there are a couple of picturesque boatyards on the southern bank.

Gulls silhouetted against the dawn light, Carmyle Weir.

As you approach Glasgow Green, the Clyde takes many twists and turns. Here, the Clyde looks back towards Rutherglen.

Left: Winter sunrise, near Dalmarnock. This site is to be redeveloped for the 2014 Commonwealth Games.

Overleaf: Peace, perfect peace, The River Clyde near Parkhead at dawn. Amazingly, several major roads are only a short distance from this spot.

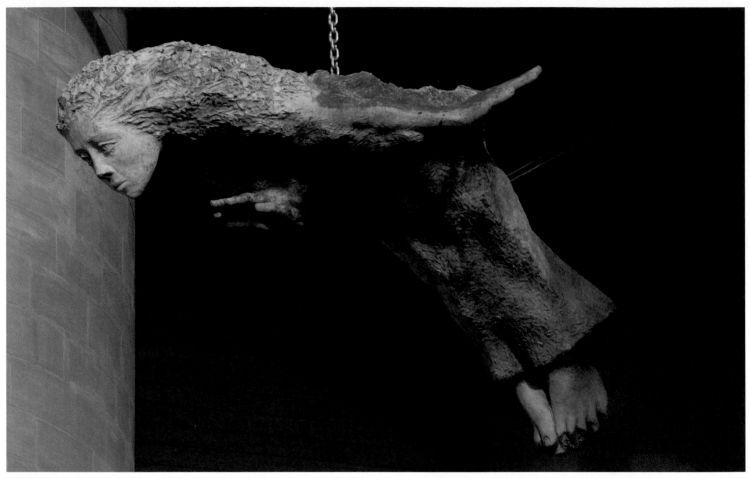

The Angel looking over New Gorbals and symbolises the rebirth of this once notorious district of Glasgow.

On the south side of the river here are extensive vegetated mounds, which are the remains of former industrial activity; waste dumped here by factories like the Clydebridge Steel Works and White's notorious chemical factory in Rutherglen. Paradoxically, because they have remained untouched and isolated, these areas are now an extensive haven for the flora and fauna that have adapted to the conditions. It has recently been proposed that the area should become Clydeside's version of the Eden Project.

One of the many striking designs to be found within the redeveloped Gorbals.

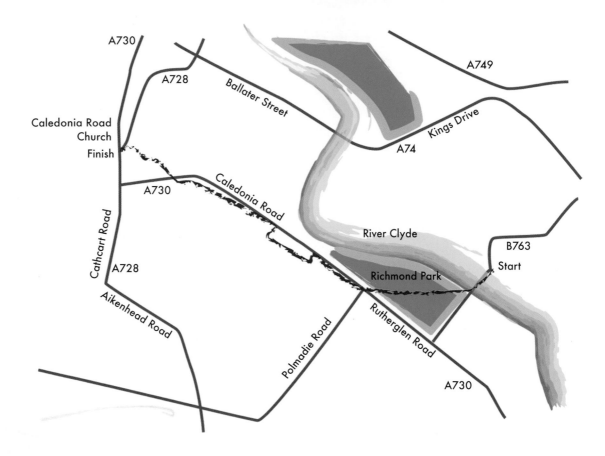

Walk: Rutherglen Bridge to the New Gorbals

The Clyde bends end at Rutherglen Bridge, just before Glasgow Green. On the south bank Shawfield Drive takes you in a couple of minutes to Shawfield Stadium, former home of Clyde FC. The football team have long moved out, but the stadium is still a popular venue for dog racing. It was built in the 1930s and in its day was probably the finest art deco sports venue in Scotland. The practised eye will still notice the period details despite the stadium falling on hard times.

Opposite is Richmond Park, whose pond hosts a very active model boat club. The Polmadie Burn runs through the park in a deep dark glade, to emerge into the Clyde opposite Glasgow Green. On the south side of the park, Rutherglen Road soon brings you to the Southern Necropolis, Glasgow's City of the Dead for those on the south side of the river. With its stunning entrance gate designed by Charles Wilson, it contains many graves of eminent Glaswegians, including Sir Thomas Lipton and Alexander 'Greek' Thomson. A little further along are the dramatic remains of Thomson's Caledonia Road Church, which seems to complement the wonderful modernist architecture of the New Gorbals hereabouts. Return to Rutherglen Bridge by a perambulation through the New Gorbals, which might overcome any reservations you have about modern architecture. The round trip is four to five miles and takes two hours.

The regeneration of the Gorbals continues and was summed up perfectly by a local, who commented when I took this photograph 'Who would have ever thought it? A park in the Gorbals.' The park is overlooked by the impressive ruin of the Caladonia Road Church.

Glasgow Green

'The Green' is a virtually flat piece of land between the bends in the Clyde and Glasgow city centre, and is endowed by nature with little in the way of eye-catching features – apart from the river itself. Yet there can be few other 100 acres or so of ground anywhere that can match the richness in historical associations possessed by Glasgow Green, nor have such wealth and variety in the way of a built legacy. Armies have marched across the Green and camped on it and it has been the scene of great social festivities and sporting events, as well as of epoch-making political meetings. The Green can also stake a claim to be the birthplace of the Industrial Revolution, many monuments and relics of which lie within a short radius. The skyline from the Green encompasses buildings of architectural merit and historical significance from the 17th century to the 21st.

The Glasgow Weir, reflected on a calm, spring morning, draws the eye to the diversity of Glasgow's architecture.

The St Andrew's
Suspension Bridge.

The River Clyde at Glasgow Green is home to many boating clubs.

From the Clyde Walkway the Green is entered at Allan's Pen gate. This commemorates Allan, a local factory owner in the early 1800s, who covered over the path with a 'pen' to direct walkers from his property. Local weavers refused to work for him in protest, but the Clyde had the last word, sweeping the pen away in a flood. A bit further along the Walkway is joined, over the fine 1850s St Andrew's Suspension Bridge, by a path from the redeveloped Gorbals district. Alongside the river hereabouts are the premises of several boating clubs, and just a short distance away is the headquarters of the Glasgow Humane Society, a charity devoted to river rescue. Just before the Walkway leaves the Green, it passes the Glasgow Weir, which may look like a bridge but is a fine example of Victorian flood control engineering. A delightful smell often pervades the river here, and it comes from the grain distillery across the river in the Gorbals.

The steeple of St Andrew's in the square rises above some more modern housing.

But to take the Walkway through the Green and miss its many other attractions would be a folly. We need to go back to these attractions and back to the history of the Green itself, which, among its many other accolades, deserves that of the oldest public park in Britain. The origins of the Green date back to the 15th century, when it was recognised as part of the common lands of Glasgow, where every citizen had grazing rights. This practice is still shown in early 19th-century drawings, in which, alongside the well-dressed citizens out for a stroll, the locals can be seen grazing their sheep. Once the Green was laid out as a park for the city in the 1820s by the city's Director of Public Works, James Cleland, this tradition declined, though another, of using the Green for the communal washing and bleaching of linens in the sun, continued well into the 20th century. This practice is commemorated by a set of washing poles erected when the Green was recently renovated.

Memorial to James Martin, former councillor and magistrate of Glasgow.

DRYING GREEN

For centuries, Glasgow Green served as the common washing green for the city.
With improvements in sanitation and the introduction of piped water to
peoples' homes, this tradition largely died out.
However, the Victorian clothes poles originally erected to serve the
nearby public wash houses, were still in use as late as the 1970's. One of
the more unusual rights acquired by Freemen of Glasgow is to dry
their clothes on Glasgow Green.

The drying green at Glasgow Green was for centuries used by the citizens of Glasgow to dry their washing.

Popular use of the Green continued when it became the site of the Glasgow Fair. This was originally a trading fair but over the years became identified with the local industrial workers' summer holiday and latterly consisted largely of amusement arcades (known as 'penny geggies'), performers giving shows and drinking hostelries. The term Glasgow Fair is still used for the local annual summer holiday in July. The fair declined with time, but the Green remained the recreational choice of the lower classes, and many traditional sports took place there – shinty, golf and cricket – although in the later 19th century these were eclipsed by the new pastime of football, and the great Glasgow Rangers started life 'on the green'. The use of the Green for concerts such as T in the Park and as the site of the annual International Pipe Band Competition can be seen as the continuation of this tradition.

With politicisation of the masses increasing, the Green was the scene of religious meetings, assemblies of temperance organisations and of the suffragette agitation. In 1832 an amazing 150,000 people gathered on the Green to support agitation

101

Glasgow Green is home to numerous swans, ducks and other birdlife.

for the Parliamentary Reform Act of that year. Latterly it was the focus of the working-class movement and the favoured haunt of trade unionists and political radicals such as John Maclean, who held rallies here to oppose the slaughter of World War One. Later attempts to curtail this right of assembly led to successful 'free speech' agitation on the Green in the 1930s. Again this political tradition is still alive, and almost 100,000 people gathered on the Green to protest against the invasion of Iraq.

But the Green has seen its own wars and armies. In 1679 the Covenanting army, victorious from the Battle of Drumclog, marched by this way but found Glasgow fortified against it and retreated to Bothwell, where it later faced its nemesis. In 1746 the Jacobite army, under Bonnie Prince Charlie, retreated towards *their* nemesis at Culloden through Glasgow. Charles stayed at the Shawfield mansion in the Trongate, but his army was encamped on Fleshers' Haugh, the eastern part of the Green, and here the Pretender reviewed his troops, who were diminishing in numbers and enthusiasm. The Jacobites left the city, to the relief of its burghers, who were profoundly hostile to the cause of the Stuarts. Yet events of even greater significance than this saw their origins on the Green.

Much has taken place on Glasgow Green, from protests to rock concerts.

James Watt Stone, commemorating the point where James Watt happened upon his idea for the separate condenser for the steam engine.

James Watt was an instrument mechanic at Glasgow University, which until the 1870s lay near to the Green. He was working on the repair of a model of a Newcomen engine when he took his usual lunchtime walk on the Green, and there he came up with the idea of the separate condenser for the steam engine. This development not only enabled steam power to be applied in factory production, but also paved the way for the railways and steamship navigation. A headless statue of Watt lay among the bushes of Fleshers' Haugh for many years, but in the restoration of the Green it has been recapitated and placed near to the People's Palace at the heart of the Green.

The People's Palace is a museum dedicated to the working-class history of Glasgow and is a must-see for anyone visiting the Green. It was funded by one of the late Victorian Industrial Exhibitions and was probably the earliest museum dedicated to working-class and industrial history to be built anywhere. As well as its permanent collection of industrial and social history, the Palace contains

Right: The great glass dome of the People's Palace, beautifully silhouetted at dawn.

The extravagant yet wonderfully idiosyncratic
Templeton's carpet factory.

Previous page: No visit to
Glasgow Green would be
complete without a trip to
see the People's Palace.

A detail of the elaborate
Templeton Carpet factory.

detailed information about the history of the Green and a series of leaflets describing its walks and monuments. But what would you see if you were one of those pigeons or seagulls perched on the roof of the People's Palace?

Another palace, the Doge's Palace as it is still known, or Templeton's carpet factory as it was, lies to the north-east. This must have been the most beautiful and extravagant factory in the world when it was built in 1889 to the designs of William Leiper. The polychrome tiles and terracotta brickwork were meant to recall the palace of the Venetian ruler and thus not spoil the built frontage to the Green. A nearby gate commemorates the 29 workers who were killed when the partially built construction collapsed. The whole area around the Green, Bridgeton and Calton on the north side of the Clyde, and Gorbals to the south of the river became heavily industrialised in the early 19th century, as a direct result of Watt's invention, which allowed factories to be placed anywhere by freeing them from their dependence on water power.

The Doulton Fountain is the largest surviving terracotta structure in the world.

Part of the Doulton Fountain's intricate detail

To the west of the Doge's Palace is found another of the Green's superlatives – the Doulton Victoria fountain, the largest surviving terracotta structure in the world. It stands as a paradigm for the British Empire at the date of its construction in 1888. On top sits the monarch, and below are her armed forces. Under that lie the main overseas colonies, and all is supported on a base which represents Glasgow, then the Second City of the Empire and its industrial capital. Without the ships, locomotives and other industrial goods produced by the city, it is difficult to imagine the functioning of the Empire in Victorian days.

Little remains of the fashionable houses of the bourgeoisie and the university professors of the 18th century, which at Montieth Row and Charlotte Street flanked the north side of the Green. Incredible though it sounds, Glasgow's perfect mediaeval university was demolished by the Victorians to be replaced by a railway station and marshalling yard, and the fashionable followed the new centre of learning to the West End of the city, as the East End increasingly became an overcrowded slum.

But at 52 Charlotte Street one urban villa reputedly by Robert Adam remains, and it has been restored as a hotel. Charlotte Street was, until about 1820, Glasgow's top

A break in the clouds highlights the magnificent Doulton Fountain.

The monument to William Collins, remembered for his work for the Temperance movement.

William Collins.

address, and David Dale, the founder of New Lanark cotton mills, had his urban mansion in one of those Adam buildings. Dale's house was demolished 50 years ago and is now a car park, which is surrounded by new buildings that continue westwards into Greendyke Street. Many of these were constructed as Homes for the Future for the Year of Architecture in 1999, and they show that Glasgow's architectural flair has not deserted the city.

On Greendyke Street is a former church, St Andrew's by the Green, now offices, dating from 1750. This was the first Episcopalian Church to be built in Glasgow following the Glorious Revolution of 1690, and the first to have an organ. Hence it was known as the Whistlin' Kirk (the Scots slang for an organ was 'a kist o' whistles'). The architect was expelled from the Kirk of Scotland for this outrageous piece of idolatry, but although the Kirk is gone its nickname survives in the Whistlin' Kirk pub on Greendyke Street.

A Kist o' Monuments stands at the entrance to the Green, Jocelyn's Gate commemorates the bishop of that name who gained Glasgow burgh status and the Collins Fountain stands in memory of its namesake's work for the Temperance movement. Here too stands the Maclennan Arch, which is not really a monument, being all that remains of the famed Adam brothers' Assembly Rooms. The park has other fine memorials, including – to the chagrin of London – the first Nelson's Column, constructed in 1806, and a drinking fountain to Hugh MacDonald, an early populariser of urban walking and of the Green in particular in his 1850s book *Rambles Round Glasgow*. The area around here was the main setting for the Glasgow Fair, and it was also the scene of public executions until 1865. The condemned died 'facing the monument' (Nelson's),

Previous Page: The Maclennan Arch at dusk, a magnificent entrance or exit to Glasgow Green.

and the most notable was probably James Wilson, executed in 1820 for his part in the so-called Radical War of that year.

By now we are on the riverside and back on the Clyde Walkway, which takes us by a fascinating riparian ramble to the end of this stage of our exploration, the Scottish Exhibition Conference Centre. But before heading on your urban safari you might like to seek refreshment in the Winter Gardens, yet another attraction of the Green, which is less of a park and more a microcosm of a great city. One theory as to the derivation of Glasgow's name is that it is a corruption of the Gaelic for 'dear green place'. For most Glaswegians, 'The Green' is their dear green place.

The great monolith of Nelson's Column dominates Glasgow Green.

Glasgow

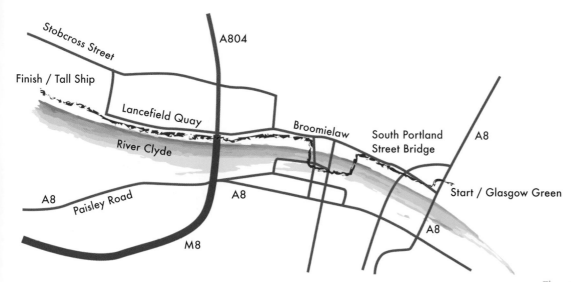

The stunning St Andrew's in the square, a recognisable landmark within Glasgow.

Walk: From the Green to the Kelvin

It is less than a couple of miles from Glasgow Green to where the River Kelvin joins the Clyde, but there is so much to see and so many possibilities for side trips that it is well to spare a few hours for the stroll.

The first sight of interest is the former Glasgow Corporation Fish Market. Dating from the 1870s, it has elaborate cast-iron doorways and is adorned with four fine sculpted seahorses on top. Rising from the middle of the building is an incongruous, much older structure, the 17th-century Merchants' or Briggait

Steeple – all that remains of the original Merchants' Guildhall and Hospital. The building is now the Briggait Centre, workshops for artists and craftspeople. Opposite on the south bank of the river rises a very different building, the Glasgow Central Mosque, built in the 1980s for the city's Muslim community.

Overleaf: Glasgow and her buildings perfectly reflected in the River Clyde on a beautiful summer's morning.

One of Carlton Place's many fine buildings.

South Portland Street Suspension Bridge, taking you across the
Clyde to the Georgian terrace of Carlton Place.

Further along Clyde Street the river is faced by many striking new flats, as the population living in the city centre increases. The South Portland Street Suspension Bridge crosses the river here, a good example of Victorian engineering and actually the oldest surviving bridge on the Glasgow section of the Clyde, dating from 1853. It is worth crossing the river here to look at Carlton Place. This Georgian terrace dating from the 1800s was the initial part of an abandoned scheme to build a quality suburb in the Gorbals. It is the finest Georgian terrace in Glasgow, and the interiors, especially at Laurieston House, are splendid. They are reputed to have been executed by the craftsmen who worked on Hampton Court.

Crossing back by the George V Bridge brings you to Glasgow's famed Broomielaw. Once this street and the

St Andrew's Cathedral.

Detail of the elaborate stonework, St Andrew's Cathedral.

Top right, right and below: Stone carving, Clydeside, Glasgow.

quays to the west were among the world's busiest shipping locations, from whence boats departed for all four corners of the globe. Today the only boat on the Broomielaw is the former Renfrew Ferry, a car ferry moved here as a floating, but static, concert venue. After years of dereliction the whole area around the Broomielaw is being re-developed as Glasgow's International Financial Services District. Today, as many people work in this sector in Glasgow as built ships in the heyday of the Clyde. But there are still many examples of the Clyde's former glories as an industrial river to examine here.

Right: The magnificent Clydeport building.

An example of the wonderful stone and ironwork to be found around Clydeside, if you look closely.

On the corner of Robertson Street and the Broomielaw is the Clydeport building, designed by John Burnet in the 1880s. Burnet also designed and oversaw much of the interior furnishing of the building and the installation of the marvellous sculptures on the exterior. The stained glass inside, representing various industrial scenes, is by Stephen Adam, the greatest Scottish stained-glass artist of the 19th century. The sculptures outside, of famous Scottish engineers and classical nautical figures such as Neptune and Triton, were composed by John Mossman and Albert Hodge. The A-listed building is still the headquarters of Clydeport (now basically a property development company rather than a maritime one) but can be visited on special open days. Further along, at James Watt Street, can be found fine Adam-style warehouses dating from the later 18th and early 19th centuries, many of which have been converted into flats.

We now approach the Kingston Bridge, built in the 1970s and at peak times one of the busiest motorway bridges in Europe. On the south bank of the river can be seen the massive palace of the former headquarters of the Scottish Wholesale Co-operative Society, completed in 1897. This grand building was reputed to be a variant of one of the unsuccessful entrants in the competition for the Glasgow City Chambers. It splendidly reflects the growing power of the co-operative movement at that time, and, alas, its subsequent decline. The building was sold and converted into luxury apartments. From the Kingston Bridge to the Kelvin River there was once a dense concentration of docks, marshalling yards and heavy industry, but none of this remains. On both banks of the river, modern apartment blocks and hotels now mingle with renovated warehouses. This section of the river ends at the Clyde Arc, the futuristic and most recent addition to Glasgow's riverscape, dubbed the Squinty Bridge by locals because of its acute-angled alignment to the river.

The Kingston Bridge at dusk: at rush hour this is one of the busiest stretches of motorway in Europe.

Glasgow built the Clyde, and the Clyde built Glasgow.

The next section of the Clyde consists of the former Queen's Dock on the northside, and Princes Dock on the south side, most of which were infilled in the 1980s and 1990s as shipping on the Clyde declined to near zero. An iconic reminder of those days is the fine Finnieston Crane just beyond the Clyde Arc. This was used mainly for loading locomotives built in Glasgow's Springburn district onto ships bound for India and elsewhere, and it has survived where most other cranes on the river went for scrap.

Another reminder of the industrial days of the Clyde is found half a mile westwards in the former Customs House, a graceful Italianate building dating from 1870. Now partly a restaurant, it is also currently the visitor centre for the *Glenlee*, the tall ship berthed nearby. Though dubbed Glasgow's ship, since it was typical of the sailing vessels carrying the city's trade in the mid-Victorian era, the Glenlee was actually built downriver in Port Glasgow. It will be a focal point of the new Riverside Museum, which is under construction from here to the River Kelvin.

A brilliant sunset silhouettes cranes on Glasgow's skyline, one of the many reminders of her industrial past.

The huge Finnieston Crane and The Armadillo, from the Clyde Arc bridge, affectionately known as the Squinty Bridge.

The Finnieston Crane and the Customs House are engineering and architectural reminders of the city's past. Its present, between these two memorials of the past, is uncompromisingly modernistic in style on both riverbanks. On the south, large areas were the scene of the Garden Festival of 1988, which represented the faltering start of the regeneration of the Clyde. Bells Bridge, built for the festival, carries you over to Pacific Quay, to the gleaming metal and glass of the new Scottish headquarters of the BBC, to the Glasgow Science centre and Imax cinema, and to the tallest construction in the city to date, the Glasgow Eye. South of these, a pleasant green area had been developed as Festival Park.

Overleaf: Pre-dawn light gives the River Clyde and her buildings a wonderful metallic finish.

On the northern bank is the Scottish Exhibition and Conference Centre (SECC). Named the Big Tin Shed by Glaswegians, it has brought massive business to the city. More loved is the adjacent Clyde Auditorium, which bears more than a passing resemblance to the Sydney Opera House and has acquired the nickname of The Armadillo. These are made a trio by the nearby hotel, clad in black glass, which gives marvellous reflections of the river and the buildings around. But even here the past raises its head: on both river banks are quaint round brick buildings, the north and south Rotundas. These were the entry points to a pedestrian and vehicle tunnel under the Clyde, built in Victorian times, and which finally closed in the 1960s. Luckily, the buildings survived closure. One is used as a casino and restaurant, while the other is awaiting redevelopment.

Finnieston Crane standing guard over the circular Rotunda casino and restaurant.

Pacific Quay perfectly reflected in the River Clyde at dawn.

Looking across Glasgow
from Pacific Quay at dusk.

Opposite: A vibrant sky
descends over Glasgow.

Overleaf: Developments here
include the relocation of both the
BBC and Scottish Television.

The futuristic façade of one of Clydeside's many modern buildings.

Glasgow's version of Sydney Opera House – The Armadillo.

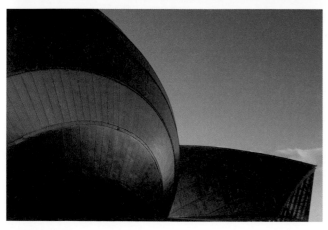

Glasgow's redevelopment of the River Clyde has given many of the buildings a much more modern look.

A good place for refreshment after your walk is the riverside decking of the City Inn, with the Finnieston Crane towering above you, looking across the river past the Clyde Arc to the south Rotunda, and west to the Armadillo and Science Centre. It's a place to ponder a great river's past, and its future. And from

The *Glenlee*, more commonly known as *The Tall Ship*, was actually built at Port Glasgow.

The iconic red funnels of the paddle steamer the *Waverley*, still regularly ferrying passengers Doon the Watter.

here you can see, below the Glasgow Eye, something in bright red, black and white colours. It is the paddle steamer the Waverley, which will accompany us on our voyage to the mouth of the river and to the Firth of Clyde.

Overleaf: A monumental sky dwarfs Glasgow's industrial landscape.

Doon the Watter 1:
The North Bank of the Clyde

For generations the Broomielaw and the Glasgow docks were not only places where imports came in and exports went out. In summer they were also the departure points for scores of paddle steamers carrying the wage slaves of Clydeside Doon the Watter to the Clyde resort villages for the annual Fair holiday. Although this tradition finally came to an end in the 1960s, one relic of those days still provides day trips on the Clyde and the Firth of Clyde in the summer months. This is the paddle steamer the *Waverley*, the only ocean-going paddle steamer left in the world. The construction of the Glasgow Arc bridge led to the moving of the ship from its former Broomielaw mooring further downriver to below the Glasgow Eye, and few would deny that these two complement each other. Anyone who is in Glasgow when the *Waverley* sails should take advantage of this unique way of seeing the river. Here we will take a virtual voyage down both banks, to Helensburgh on the north side of the Clyde and to Gourock on the south – both ports at which the much-moved vessel still calls.

A beautiful sunset over Clydebank.

Opposite page:
Top right: The mammoth Titan crane, standing overlooking the Clyde on the site of John Brown's shipyard. The crane is now a tourist attraction.

Bottom right: As in many towns on the Clyde, there is much to admire, not least the architecture. Clydebank Town Hall is a good example.

Bottom left: Old machinery, Clydebank.

Solidarity Square, Clydebank.

Dawn over the River Clyde, the hazy sunshine picking out the high-rise buildings around Clydebank.

A beautiful calm morning at Bowling Basin.

On passing the mouth of the Kelvin, the old boat itself must feel nostalgic. For it was here in 1947 at Inglis's Pointhouse shipyard that the *Waverley* was built as a replacement for a similarly named boat lost at Dunkirk. Closed in the 1960s, the site of the yard is disappearing beneath the new Riverside Museum. On past the Kelvin mouth lies Meadowside Quay, formerly the site of the massive brick granaries of the Clyde Port Authority, and now lined by megalithic new luxury flats.

Another early casualty of the contraction in Clyde shipbuilding was the Barclay Curle and Co. works, which also closed in the 1960s. But the hammerhead crane of this yard still stands by the riverside, and so too does the unusual engine works of the yard, with its mansard roof. The building is still in industrial, non-shipbuilding use.

The Kilpatrick Hills above Old Kilpatrick offer some excellent walking possibilities and some wonderful views across Glasgow...

...and (overleaf) in the other direction, the panorama along the Firth of Clyde towards Greenock is superb.

145

All along the river here were famous industrial firms, including Albion motors and Connel's shipyard. Another famous name that has gone is that of Yarrows shipyard, although the yard itself remains and is one of the last two on the Clyde. Today it is owned by BAE Systems and largely produces warships here in Scotstoun, and with 2,000 employees it is one of the largest manufacturing units left on the whole of Clydeside. But most of the great engineering works that stretched for mile after mile along the north bank of the river have closed their doors, and their demolished sites are being built over, largely to make way for new housing developments.

At Yoker we come to the last functioning Clyde ferry, no longer a car carrier but still taking bikes and pedestrians across the river to Renfrew. It is a unique relic of the days when dozens of ferries crossed the Clyde, carrying workers from their homes on one side of the river to their workplaces on the other. Now making heavy losses, the Renfrew–Yoker ferry is threatened with closure and replacement by a tunnel or bridge. After the ferry, we soon leave Glasgow and enter the riverside of Clydebank, where the rebirth of the Clyde is also underway.

As you leave the urban landscape of Glasgow, the countryside around the Clyde is at times surprisingly lush. In sharp contrast, the great concrete bulk of the Erskine Bridge spans the Clyde.

Most of the Clyde frontage here – over a mile of it – was taken up with possibly the greatest shipyard of them all. Originally Thomson's, later John Brown's, the Clydebank yard, built the best passenger ships in the world, including the *Lusitania* and the later series of Cunard 'Queen' liners. The yard operated for over a century and at its height employed almost 10,000 men. It was a target for the Luftwaffe during World War Two, when Clydebank was blitzed, leading to the loss of 600 lives and almost all the housing stock being destroyed or damaged.

The yard itself was never hit, though the local Auchentoshan Distillery was, and the ignited whisky gave the German planes enough light to bomb the town. Auchentoshan still produces a very fine Lowland Malt, but John Brown's body gave up the ghost and the yard lay mouldering for almost 20 years. Now it is the site of the futuristic Clydebank College and has been designated for housing developments. A reminder of the yard is given by the huge Titan crane, which has been retained and restored as a tourist attraction. It is the biggest crane left on the Clyde.

Mar Hall Hotel, perfectly positioned on the banks of the Clyde.

Sunlight after a passing storm lights up the distillery at Auchentoshan.

Far left: The distinctive pagodas of Auchentoshan distillery, purveyors of an excellent Lowland Malt.

Left: Old barrels, Auchentoshan Distillery.

Looking along the Clyde from above the village of Old Kilpatrick.

Looking towards the Erskine Bridge at dusk from Bowling Basin.

We leave Clydebank on passing another modern building, the Golden Jubilee Hospital, which occupies much of the site of another shipyard now gone, Beardmore's Dalmuir yard. The hospital was originally the HCI, a private venture intended to attract affluent foreign patients for treatment. It failed and was taken into the National Health Service a few years ago. On leaving Clydebank, the river bank is occupied by a series of bonded warehouses up to the last of the bridges over the Clyde, the Erskine Bridge, which replaced the ferry here in the early 1970s.

The next item of interest is the junction of the Clyde with the Forth and Clyde Canal at Bowling. It was near here that the Romans' Antonine Wall reached the west coast. The deepening of the Clyde so that it could take large vessels was a mid-19th-century development, and before that the main conduit for Scotland's trade was the Forth and Clyde canal, whose western terminus was at Bowling. From here, shipping carried freight to Glasgow and then on to the east coast at Bo'ness. Bowling Basin is a fascinating place, a cluster of canal locks, former locksmen's housing and the old Customs House.

Some boats have been left in a state of disrepair.

The canal was closed in the 1960s, and as the basin decayed it became ever more picturesque, with many people settling there in boathouses. The reopening of the Forth and Clyde canal has been a great tourist and recreational boon, but in the tidying up of the Bowling Basin, something of its popular charm is being lost.

Bowling has been left to decay in recent years but, like much of the industrial Clyde, it is being cleaned up and repackaged.

Colourful boats, Bowling.

Even though Bowling Basin has seen better days, it still has a certain appeal. For example, like these old sheds…

…and the decaying remains of this old wooden pier.

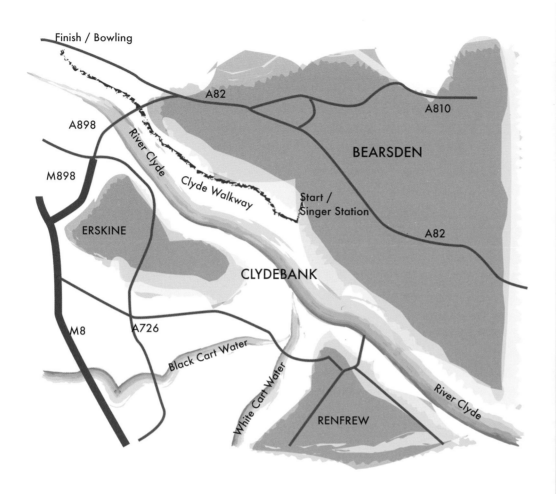

The perfect arc of a rainbow over Dumbarton Rock and her castle.

Walk: Clydebank to Bowling Basin

From Singer station in Clydebank, Kilbowie Road leads a quarter of a mile south to the Forth and Clyde Canal. Opened in the 1790s, it gave access from the Clyde on the west coast of Scotland to the Forth on the east, and was one of the arteries of the Industrial Revolution. It closed in the 1960s but was successfully re-opened recently as a recreational and tourist resource. The former towpath has been developed as a cycle track, and it gives excellent walking on its southern bank. To the north of the canal here is found a

modern business park. This was the former site of the giant Singer sewing machine factory, whose clock tower was visible for miles. In the 1950s it was the largest factory in Europe, with 17,000 workers and its own railway station, which still retains the name.

The canal is pleasantly wooded on both banks here and soon crosses Dumbarton Road, running west between that busy thoroughfare and the River Clyde to the south. Between river and canal at this point can be seen the striking modern Golden Jubilee Hospital, and then an industrial estate, once the site of Beardmore's Dalmuir shipyard.

The walk continues through delightful countryside, and the canal makes its way under a swing bridge before passing under the more massive structures of the Erskine Bridge. The canal also crosses over the Dalnottar Burn here, and between canal and river at this point is a salt wetland, a Site of Special Scientific Interest.

Soon after that, Bowling is reached: this is the terminal point of the canal, where it enters the Clyde. Just here are the first locks on the canal and a set of fine lock-keepers' houses. Then you pass

Dumbarton Castle, the old military capital of the ancient kingdom of Strathclyde.

Cannon, Dumbarton Castle.

under a railway bridge, to where the restored former Customs House provides a fine counterpoint to the colourful and varied mass of boats, and the view downriver is great. It is about four miles from Singer station to Bowling, and it is an easy, flat walk, which takes a couple of lazy hours. You can retrace your steps to Clydebank for an extra bit of exercise, or simply catch the train back to Glasgow at Bowling station, five minutes from the basin.

Downstream from here the river widens, becoming more of a tidal estuary, but it is still the Clyde. It was here that the first steamboat in the world, the Comet, the great-great-grandfather of the Waverley in a way, underwent its trials in 1812. There is a very famous painting by John Knox, called The First Steamboat on the Clyde, which shows the view downriver at this time. Then, and now, it is a thing of great beauty.

Holding the eye of the viewer is a huge rock at the edge of the river, a couple of miles from Bowling – or rather a double volcanic plug. This is Dumbarton Rock, which can claim to be the longest continually occupied site in the British Isles, and certainly one of the most dramatic.

The eye-catching remains of Cardross Church.

This is Dun Breatann, the Fort of the Britons and the military capital of the ancient Kingdom of Strathclyde, dating back to possibly the seventh century. (The ecclesiastical centre of this kingdom was in Govan.) Strathclyde stretched southwards to the present Lake District and northwards to the head of Loch Lomond. Strathclyde eventually became one of the constituent parts of the Kingdom of Scotland, which emerged in the 10th and 11th centuries, but Dumbarton Rock and its castle remained an important centre of military power thereafter. It was taken by opponents of Mary, Queen of Scots, in the religious wars of the 16th century when the attackers scaled the cliffs – something modern climbers might hesitate to do. Thereafter it went into decay, though it was re-fortified during the French Revolutionary Wars around 1800. The mansion gatehouse visible from the river dates from this period. As befits its importance, Dumbarton Castle is a Scheduled Ancient Monument under the care of Historic Scotland.

To the west of Dumbarton Rock, the town that got its name from the ancient fortress had another 'castle', the former Hiram Walker grain distillery. This huge brick building was constructed in the 1930 so that Walker, a Canadian, could supply enough hooch to prohibition America. At that time it was the largest grain distillery in the world. Sadly, the distillery is closed and much of it has been demolished, but the very fine main tower of the building still stands as a significant landmark, and it is hoped that it can be redeveloped in some way.

Dumbarton was also a shipyard town, and the local firm of Denny's dominated the place for 150 years. Their yard was near the Leven's mouth, just below the castle, and must have been the most scenic shipyard in the world. Denny's specialised in medium-sized craft and built many paddle steamers, as well as completing the famous Cutty Sark sailing ship.

A wonderful dawn sky at Ardmore Point.

Ardmore Point offers an outstanding viewpoint across the Clyde to Helensburgh, and beyond to the great hills and mountains of Cowal.

The yard was always in the forefront of marine innovation, and astonishingly its model ship tank, which in the 1880s was the first civilian testing tank in the world, still survives and is open to visitors. As long as a football field, this is a unique must-see. The tank avoided closure with the yard in the 1960s, as it was used by other shipbuilders and later by university engineering students. It is now a detached part of the Scottish Maritime Museum.

Clocktower, Helensburgh.

Bust of John Logie Baird, inventor of the television, who was born in Helensburgh in 1888.

After Dumbarton we leave the industrial river, and the Clyde's banks are increasingly the location of suburban Victorian and Edwardian villas and hotels. This development reaches its culmination in Helensburgh, a town built with no other function than as a dormitory for businessmen and retirees from Glasgow, and as a Clyde holiday resort. It was originally laid out as a planned town by Colquhoun of Luss in the 1770s and at first grew slowly.

Henry Bell, the designer of the Comet, came to live here in 1800. His motivation for developing steam navigation was to bring people from Glasgow to his wife's hydropathic hotel in Helensburgh. Bell became the town's first Provost and is commemorated by a monument on the promenade. The railway arrived in the 1850s, and then the town grew rapidly.

For a quiet, wee place it has many historical associations. Also on the seafront near Bell's monument is one to John Logie Baird, pioneer of television and radar, who was born in Helensburgh in 1888. The village's seafront has the feel of a Clyde resort, with many cafés and amusement venues, but behind this lies a collection of some of the first villas of the Victorian era, built by some of the most noted architects. One stands out head and shoulders above the rest: Hill House, designed in 1904 by the Glasgow architect Charles Rennie Mackintosh, and possibly his finest piece of domestic architecture.

The distinctive style of the Charles Rennie Mackintosh-designed Hill House, a major tourist attraction.

Late-evening sunshine strikes the attractive frontage of Helensburgh, still a popular destination for day trippers.

The Glasgow publisher W.W. Blackie had decided on a move to Helensburgh and commissioned Mackintosh to build this house, a combination of art nouveau and Scots vernacular, leaving all details – including furnishings – to the architect. Tens of thousands come yearly to be enthralled by this masterpiece, now in the care of the National Trust for Scotland.

In the holiday season the *Waverley* still calls occasionally at Helensburgh, stopping at Craigendoran Pier on the village's east side. And from Helensburgh's own central pier, a Strathclyde Passenger Transport ferry plies in summer to Gourock, near Greenock. It could be argued that this is a Clyde ferry, and it could soon be the last of them, but since it takes a triangular route from Helensburgh to Gourock via Kilcreggan in Cowal, I personally feel that this ferry strays out of the waters of the River Clyde proper into the waters of the Firth of Clyde improper. But notwithstanding this reservation, a summer trip to Helensburgh by train from Glasgow, followed by the ferry via Kilcreggan to Gourock, and the return train journey thence by rail to Glasgow, is as fine a way of seeing the Clyde as is a trip on the *Waverley* itself. But let us here instead return telepathically from Helensburgh to the *Waverley's* berth at the Glasgow Eye, and take a virtual trip down the south bank of the Clyde.

The Strathclyde Passenger Transport ferry leaves Helenburgh at sunset, its destination, via Kilcreggan, being Gourock on the other side of the Clyde.

Doon the Watter 2:
The South Bank of the Clyde

At the time of writing, the redevelopment of the south bank of the river stops suddenly just beyond the Glasgow Eye, where there is a large area of derelict land. But this is worth examination as it consists of the former Glasgow Graving Docks, and is one of the few A-listed industrial monuments to exist on the Clyde. These dry docks were, at their height, the largest in the world, capable of taking the biggest ships afloat for repair and repainting. The sluice gates of the docks are still in position, as are many other aspects of the site, including its derelict offices. The bold who wander around here, wondering at the construction, enjoy a fascinating experience. These docks are due for redevelopment in a controversial scheme which, though it will retain many features such as capstans and cobbles, will see all but one of the docks infilled.

The A-listed Graving docks, in sharp contrast with the shiny new architecture of Pacific Quay a short distance away.

This is the famed Govan district of Glasgow, once the capital of world shipbuilding. Yards such as Harland and Wolff, as well as Stephen's, have all gone, but the Fairfield yard is still in operation as another arm of BAE Systems and employs about 1,500 men. The yard is approached soon after the Graving docks, and a housing estate, built on the site of the former Harland and Wolff shipyard, is passed. But just before that is an open space where the former Govan to Patrick ferry went. In Roman times, the Clyde could be crossed here on stepping stones, something that was possible even in the 18th century.

Sandwiched between this open space and the BAE Systems yard, the outline of a church can be discerned on the skyline. This is Govan Old Church, which was built when Govan was an expanding burgh in the later 19th century. It was at least the third church to be built here since the Reformation, but the site's religious associations go back much further. Almost 1,500 years of Christian worship has taken place here, and it was a pre-Christian religious site before that.

The graveyard has many interesting memorials dating from the 17th century onwards, when Govan was a weaving and salmon-fishing settlement. But the great Glory of Govan is contained within the church, consisting of around 30 early Christian incised stones dating from the ninth century onwards, and including the wonderful Govan sarcophagus. Once reputed to be that of St Constantine, it is now thought to be the burial casket for a noble of the Strathclyde Kingdom, of which kingdom Govan was in all probability the leading religious centre.

Right: War memorial, Govan.

Opposite, top left: Graffiti, Graving docks.

Opposite, bottom: Centuries of history lie within the walls of Govan Old Kirk.

BAE Systems shipyard at dusk, viewed from across the water at Renfrew. The yard is one of the few shipyards still operating on the Clyde.

Following on from the BAE yard there is once more an undeveloped area, the location of the former Stephen's yard, and a workaday series of sites, including Glasgow's main sewage works at Shieldhall, before we come to the boundaries of the city in the King George V Dock. This is the only operative dockyard within Glasgow's boundaries today. The site of Govan Old has been a temple to many religious creeds, and at Braehead, which lies within Renfrew, we come to a temple of the modern religion of shopping. Although this site is like so many others of its kind, it does include the Clyde-Built facility, which is another detached part of the Scottish Maritime Museum, and this contains much interesting history of the shipbuilding and mercantile traditions of the Clyde. It is possible to catch a river ferry at the Broomielaw in Glasgow and sail down to Braehead.

After passing the Renfrew–Yoker ferry on its southern shore, the river is then joined by the waters of the Black Cart, into which the huge ships from John Brown's in Clydebank were launched. The north side of the river is built up for several miles here, but on the south side industry and habitation are replaced by semi-open countryside down to and beyond the Erskine Bridge, with pleasant views southwards to the hills of Renfrewshire. If feels at this point as if urban industrial Clydeside has been left behind, until Port Glasgow is neared.

The Yoker Swan and Renfrew Rose still ferry 150,000 passengers the 200 yards across the Clyde each year. It is one of the oldest passenger ferry services.

Even with the high volume of passengers using the service, the Renfrew–Yoker ferry is sadly threatened with closure.

The Ferry Inn, Clyde Street.

Had you sailed Doon the Watter 30 or 40 years ago, this last stretch of the Clyde on the south shore, between Port Glasgow and Greenock, would have presented itself as a forest of cranes, since this area was second only to Glasgow itself as a world shipbuilding centre. Yards such as Scott's of Greenock and Lithgows of Port Glasgow were among the biggest and most advanced in the world in their heyday, and 15,000 men found work in these and other local yards. Today it is as if they had never been. The only surviving parts of a once mighty industry are a small shipyard with about 200 men in Port Glasgow and a ship repair facility in Greenock with somewhat more of a workforce. The yards have been flattened, sadly, including the giant Goliath crane at Lithgows yard, the biggest ever built in Scotland and a notable landmark until recently. But the prospect of the skyline of these two towns, from river or shore, remains an engrossing one.

Dramatic skies silhouette a tug, dwarfed by the huge ship it drags up the Clyde.

The River Clyde still sees plenty of traffic.

Beautiful, warm, evening sunshine emphasises the cornfields at Inchinnan, with the Titan crane at Clydebank in the distance.

The subtle colours of frost-covered leaves below the Erskine Bridge.

Late-evening sunshine highlights the great
concrete supports of the Erskine Bridge.

Rising to 38m above the Clyde, the bridge offers a wonderful
vantage point to view the skyline of Glasgow as well as beautiful sunsets (overleaf).

Newark Castle, built in 1478 by the Maxwell Family.

Right at the shoreline as Port Glasgow is approached lies Newark Castle. It is surprising that this building, uninhabited for three centuries, survives in so complete a form. The land on both sides was occupied from the 1800s by shipyards, and the building survived since no one bothered to knock it down. The oldest part is the 15th-century tower built by the Maxwells, the local lairds, and in the later 16th century a Renaissance fortified house was added by Patrick Maxwell, a man whose cruel and dark deeds escaped punishment due to his close connection with James VI. It is one of the best examples of a fortified house in the west of Scotland, but its unique feature is the dookit (dovecot), which stands prominently on the east side of the castle. Here, pigeons were bred for food. Further de-industrialisation may soon leave the castle as it originally stood, in splendid isolation.

Port Glasgow was developed as Glasgow's port after the Union of 1707, trading especially with the sugar and tobacco plantations of the Americas. As it prospered, the town grew to independent status and was made a burgh in 1775.

A break in the clouds switches the sun's spotlight onto Dumbarton Rock from West Ferry.

From the sea or the road through the town a fine spire can be seen, leading heavenwards, and this belongs to the Burgh Hall, built in 1815 in the Neo-classical style by David Hamilton, possibly the country's leading architect at that time. It now houses the local library. Port Glasgow gradually lost its trading position to Greenock, and then to Glasgow itself, but as trade declined industry increased, especially shipbuilding. Indeed, it was at John Wood's yard in Port Glasgow that the world's first ocean-going steam-driven vessel was launched in 1812. A full-scale replica of the Comet was built by the apprentices of the Lithgow shipyard in the 1960s and stands a little way from the former Burgh Hall.

The lovely steeple of Port Glasgow's former Burgh Hall.

The Comet, a full-scale replica of the first ocean-going steam-driven vessel, sits proudly at Port Glasgow's refurbished waterfront.

Port Glasgow merges seamlessly into Greenock, where the James Watt dock is still used for shipping traffic on a modest scale. All around here are redevelopments of housing, offices and hotels, but the main sight is the huge, derelict complex of the former Greenock sugar warehouses at the dockside. At first sight this might appear an eyesore, but look carefully. These are beautifully constructed brick buildings, adorned with many ornamental brick features and fine overhanging gables. Though long disused and damaged by fire, these remains are as striking and as historically important as any castle or stately home. Indeed, they are recognised by UNESCO as one of the 'most endangered' significant industrial sites in the world. Demolition would be a tragedy, and recently funds have been set aside for its preservation.

Greenock is a town in a near-perfect situation. Across the Clyde are the mountains of the Cowal peninsula, and behind the town rise the bonny hills of Renfrewshire. It was also, in its day, a town of fabulous wealth and great poverty.

The tide is out at Langbank as the sun dips below the Cowal Hills.

Old Pier at dusk, Port Glasgow.

Left: Stormy skies and choppy waters.

The orange afterglow of sunset outlines the landscape of the Clyde.

Overleaf: A monumental sky dwarfs the Cowal Hills.

Looking across Greenock and the Clyde to the Cowal Peninsula.

The wealth was initially based on the colonial trade, before moving to shipbuilding and engineering. West of the town towards Gourock lies the large, planned area of Victorian villas, which testifies to the prosperity of Greenock's middle classes; no other Clyde town – bar Glasgow itself – has such a display of wealth. But Greenock also excels in its civic buildings, which are on a grand scale, such as the Tontine Hotel and the Woods Mariners Home. But the two greatest buildings lie in the town centre.

The Town Hall was built in 1886 at a cost of £100,000 and beyond Glasgow City Chambers is the finest on Clydeside. It is topped by the graceful, pencil-thin Victoria Tower, which at 245ft is meant to be seen by all on land and sea as a symbol of the town's pride. A statue of James Watt, Greenock's most famous son, stands outside the building. Even more impressive is the Greenock Customs House, built in 1818 in a classical revival style by William Burn. The traveller William Cobbett rightly described this building as a 'palace' – as indeed befitted the town that for a century was Scotland's main port, for the import and export of both goods and people. Greenock still

The impressive architecture of Greenock, with the remarkable 245ft structure of the town hall as its centrepiece.

has a maritime trade, though it is not what it was, and while part of the Customs House is retained for its original function, the rest has become a museum.

Past the Customs House we come to what is now a very unusual sight on the Clyde – working cranes. These are at the Clydeport container base, which handles imports and the manufactured exports Scotland still produces. Large ocean cruise liners also use this facility, since it is one of the few deep enough to berth them, keeping Greenock's maritime traditions going. Past Clydeport, Greenock Esplanade stretches westwards, with the villas of the Victorians on the left, and Helensburgh and Kilcreggan seen across the Clyde on the right. To the south of the villas lies Lyle Hill, near the top of which stands the Free French Memorial, dedicated to those of the Free French Navy who were based in Greenock during the war, many of whom gave their lives in the fight against Nazism. You can drive to the top of Lyle Hill and admire the view down the Firth of Clyde and back up the river itself, but there is a better vantage point.

The vantage point of Lyle Hill provides a fantastic view as the River Clyde reaches her journey's end, flowing into the Firth of Clyde.

From Cornalees the moorland track of two miles takes you back over the hills to Overton. From the high vantage point above Overton the spires and cranes of Greenock are wondrous to behold. Dumbarton, with its castle, and Ben Lomond far behind can be seen on a clear day, and the roving eye can follow the River Clyde out into the Firth and the wide world, and backwards towards its source, where we started this journey.